W9-CMZ-992

LIGHTNING
BOLT
BOOKS™

Silver and Gold Everywhere

Kristin Sterling

Lerner Publications Company
Minneapolis

Dedicated to teachers everywhere—you are worth your weight in gold

Copyright © 2010 by Lerner Publishing Group, Inc.

All rights reserved. International copyright secured. No part of this book may be reproduced, stored in a retrieval system, or transmitted in any form or by any means—electronic, mechanical, photocopying, recording, or otherwise—without the prior written permission of Lerner Publishing Group, Inc., except for the inclusion of brief quotations in an acknowledged review.

Lerner Publications Company
A division of Lerner Publishing Group, Inc.
241 First Avenue North
Minneapolis, MN 55401 U.S.A.

Website address: www.lernerbooks.com

Library of Congress Cataloging-in-Publication Data

Sterling, Kristin.
    Silver and Gold Everywhere / by Kristin Sterling.
        p.   cm. — (Lightning bolt books™—Colors everywhere)
    Includes index.
    ISBN 978-0-7613-4593-0 (lib. bdg. : alk. paper)
    1. Silver—Juvenile literature. 2. Gold—Juvenile literature. 3. Colors—Juvenile literature.
    I. Title.
    QC495.5.S747 2010
    535.6—dc22   2009017954

Manufactured in the United States of America
1 — BP — 12/15/09

Contents

A Rich World

Colors are all around us. They are found in nature and in things made by people.

Silver and gold are unique colors. They are named after metals.

Some U.S. coins are silver or gold.

Silver and gold metals are found in the earth. Rainwater carries bits of gold into rivers and streams.

This father and daughter pan for gold in a river.

It is easy to melt and shape these metals. **They are made into jewelry or coins.**

This bar of gold is melted so it can be made into other gold things.

Sasha is wearing a necklace and bracelet made of gold. She also has gold shoes.

People have used gold in decorations for a long time.

Ancient Egyptians made golden masks.

This golden mask was made for the ancient Egyptian ruler King Tut.

This knife, fork, and spoon
are made of silver.
Do you have
silverware?

Many churches and temples are decorated with gold and silver. This church has a golden dome.

This is Saint Isaac's Cathedral in Russia.

The silver maple is a type of tree. Its leaves look silver when they wave in the sunlight.

The front of a silver maple leaf is dark green. The back looks silvery green, especially in sunlight.

Goldenrods are
flowers with a
deep yellow color.
You can see
them when you
go hiking.

Shades of Silver and Gold

Silver and gold come in different shades. Some shades are shiny, and some are not.

Metallic gold is shiny. Kevin is playing metallic gold cymbals.

Have you ever seen a gold-colored instrument?

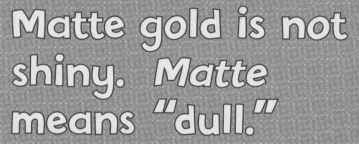

Matte gold is not shiny. *Matte* means "dull."

This shirt is matte gold.

Gold is a common color for sports teams.

Metallic silver shines just like metallic gold. This building is a metallic silver color.

The Chrysler Building is one of New York City's most famous skyscrapers.

Matte silver does not shine.

You can draw with
matte silver crayons
or colored pencils.

Colorful Sayings

People use many sayings
about silver and gold.
Maybe you say them too!

"All that glitters is not gold" means that things are not always what they seem.

The mineral pyrite is known as fool's gold. People often mistake it for real gold.

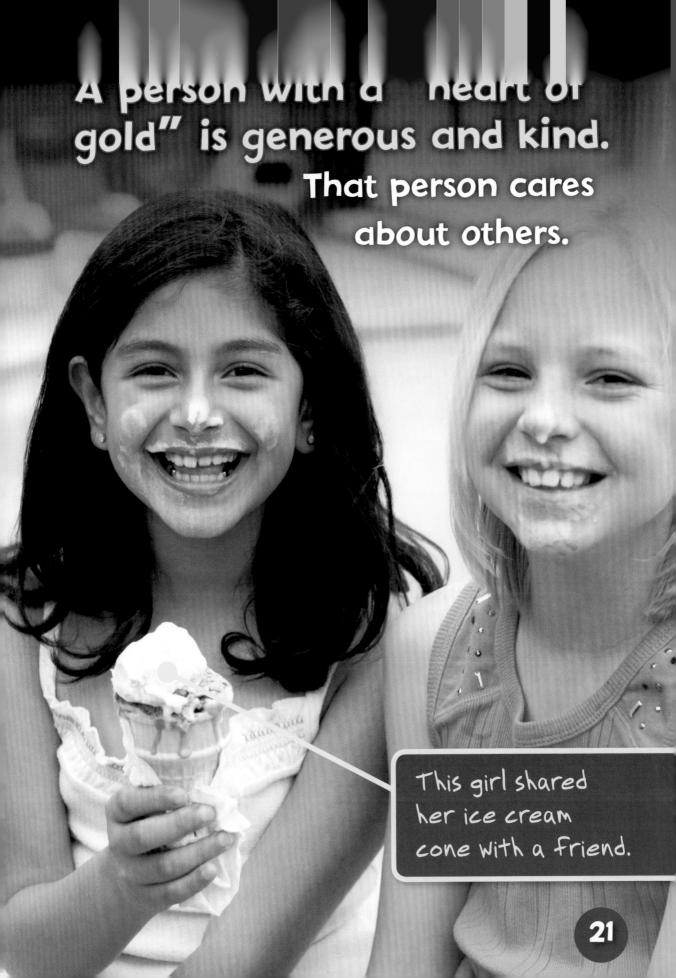

A person with a "heart of gold" is generous and kind. That person cares about others.

This girl shared her ice cream cone with a friend.

"Every cloud has a silver lining" means that hard times will lead to something better.

What is lighting up this cloud from behind?

We Love Gold

Josh loves the color gold.
His dog is a golden retriever.
They love to play together.

Greta won a gold medal in a gymnastics competition.

She wears a golden locket
around her neck.

Greta and Josh are fans of the Golden Gophers football team.

Golden Gophers fans wear their team's color at a football game. The Golden Gophers play for the University of Minnesota.

what is your favorite color?

Fun Facts

- Gold and silver coins were used as money for many years. Modern coins are made of other metals.

- Gold can be pounded into a thin sheet called gold leaf. Gold leaf can be used to decorate books, furniture, and artwork.

- In the Olympic Games, athletes win gold medals for first place. They win silver medals for second place. They win bronze medals for third place.

- Couples celebrate silver anniversaries when they have been married for twenty-five years. They celebrate gold anniversaries when they have been married for fifty years.

- People have golden birthdays when they turn the same age as their birth date. If you're turning eight and you were born on the eighth day of the month, it's your golden birthday!

- Dentists use gold for fillings and crowns. Have you ever seen a gold tooth?

Glossary

ancient: from a very long time ago

decorate: to add something beautiful to a place

dome: a roof shaped like half a ball

matte: dull, or not shiny

metallic: shiny

shade: the darkness of a color

unique: one of a kind

Further Reading

Edwards, Ron, and James Gladstone. *Gold*. New York: Crabtree Publishing, 2004.

Enchanted Learning: Color Wheel and Color Mixing
http://www.enchantedlearning.com/art/Colormixing.shtml

Gold—History for Kids!
http://www.historyforkids.org/learn/science/mining/gold.htm

Gold Rush—PBS KIDS GO!
http://pbskids.org/wayback/goldrush/index.html

Hamanaka, Sheila. *All the Colors of the Earth*. New York: Morrow Junior Books, 1994.

Ross, Kathy. *Kathy Ross Crafts Colors*. Minneapolis: Millbrook Press, 2003.

Index

Photo Acknowledgments

The images in this book are used with the permission of: © Chitra Tatachar/
Dreamstime.com, p. 1; © Dmitriy Chistoprudov/Dreamstime.com, p. 2 (top);
© Cammeraydave/Dreamstime.com, p. 2 (bottom); © iStockphoto.com/Maria Pavlova,
p. 4; © Tetra Images/Getty Images, p. 5; © Steve Vidler/SuperStock, p. 6; © Cicero Dias
Viegas/Tips Italia/Photolibrary, p. 7; © Joel Sartore/National Geographic/Getty
Images, p. 8; © Rosemary Calvert/Photographer's Choice/Getty Images, p. 9;
© iStockphoto.com/Alain Couillaud, p. 10; © Sailorr/Dreamstime.com, p. 11; © Marta
Johnson, p. 12; © Sonya Etchison/Dreamstime.com, p. 13; © Supernova/Photodisc/Getty
Images, p. 14; © Thomas Northcut/Digital Vision/Getty Images, p. 15; © James Baigrie/
Taxi/Getty Images, p. 16; © Shiningcolors/Dreamstime.com, p. 17; © vario images GmbH
& Co. KG/Alamy, p. 18; © iStockphoto.com/Martin McCarthy, p. 19; © age fotostock/
SuperStock, p. 20; © Somos/Veer/Getty Images, p. 21; © Unopix/Dreamstime.com, p. 22;
© tbkmedia.de/Alamy, p. 23; © Image Source/Getty Images, p. 24; © iStockphoto.com/
webking, p. 25; © Doug Pensinger/Getty Images, p. 26; © Goodshoot/Photolibrary,
p. 27; © Tom Grill/Iconica/Getty Images, p. 28; © Mark Huls/Dreamstime.com, p. 29;
© Mikhail Blajenov/Dreamstime.com, p. 30.

Cover: © Debra Boast/Dreamstime.com (shoes); © Mikhail Blajenov/Dreamstime.com
(fish); © Vahid Ruzibayev/Dreamstime.com (tube); © Hideki Yoshihara/Aflo/Getty
Images (medals); © iStockphoto.com/Martin McCarthy (rings); © Todd Strand/
Independent Picture Service (paint strips).